Animal Poems
for Children

Animal Poems
for Children

selected by DeWITT CONYERS ❧ *illustrated by* ANN SCHWENINGER

GOLDEN PRESS • NEW YORK
Western Publishing Company, Inc., Racine, Wisconsin

ACKNOWLEDGMENTS

The editor and publisher have made every effort to trace the ownership of all copyrighted material and to secure permission from holders of the copyrights. In the event of any questions arising as to the use of any material, the editor and publisher, while expressing regret for inadvertent error, will be pleased to make the necessary corrections in future printings. Thanks are due to the following authors, publishers, and agents for permission to use the material indicated.

Basil Blackwell for "The Happy Sheep" by Wilfred Thorley from *The Merry Go Round*, and for "The Rabbit" by Edith King from *Fifty New Poems for Children*.

Thomas Y. Crowell for "The Ducks" by Alice Wilkins from *The Golden Flute: An Anthology of Poetry for Young Children*, selected by Alice Hubbard and Adeline Babbitt. Copyright 1932, 1960, by Harper & Row, Publishers, Inc. A John Day Book. By permission of Thomas Y. Crowell, Publishers.

Hamish Hamilton Ltd for "The Turtle" by Jack Prelutsky from *Zoo Doings and Other Poems*. Published by Hamish Hamilton Ltd in the UK and British Commonwealth.

Harper & Row, Publishers, Inc., (for text) and World's Work Ltd for "Sunning" from *Crickety Cricket!: The Best-Loved Poems of James S. Tippett*. Originally published in *A World To Know* by James S. Tippett. Copyright 1933, by Harper & Row, Publishers, Inc. Renewed 1966 by Martha K. Tippett. By permission of Harper & Row, Publishers, Inc. Published in the UK and British Commonwealth by World's Work Ltd.

David Higham Associates Limited for "Mice and Cat" by Clive Sansom from *The Golden Unicorn*, published by Methuen & Co., Ltd.

Alfred A. Knopf, Inc. for "Snail", copyright 1947, by Langston Hughes. Reprinted from *Selected Poems of Langston Hughes*, by Langston Hughes, by permission of Alfred A. Knopf, Inc.

J. B. Lippincott and Harold Ober Associates Incorporated for "Mrs. Peck-Pigeon" from *Eleanor Farjeon's Poems for Children*. Originally published in *Over the Garden Wall* by Eleanor Farjeon. Copyright 1933, 1961, by Eleanor Farjeon. Reprinted by permission of J. B. Lippincott, Publishers and Harold Ober Associates Incorporated.

Macmillan Publishing Co., Inc. for "The Swallows" from *Summer Green* by Elizabeth Coatsworth, copyright 1948 by Macmillan Publishing Co., Inc., renewed 1976 by Elizabeth Coatsworth Beston; and for "The Turtle," (text only) from *Toucans Two and Other Poems* by Jack Prelutsky, copyright © 1967, 1970, by Jack Prelutsky. Reprinted with permission of Macmillan Publishing Co., Inc.

Mary Britton Miller for "Foal" and "Cat", from *Menagerie*, copyright 1928. Reprinted by permission of James N. Miller.

William Jay Smith and Delacorte Press for "Opossum" excerpted from the book *Laughing Time, Nonsense Poems* by William Jay Smith. Copyright © 1953, 1955, 1956, 1957, 1959, 1968, 1974, 1977, 1980, by William Jay Smith. Reprinted by permission of Delacorte Press/Seymour Lawrence and William Jay Smith.

Viking Penguin, Inc. for "The Firefly" from *Under the Tree* by Elizabeth Madox Roberts. Copyright 1922, by B. W. Huebsch, copyright renewed 1950 by Ivor Roberts. Reprinted by permission of Viking Penguin, Inc.

Helen Wing and Rand McNally & Company for "Crickets", from *Child Life* magazine, copyright 1925, 1953, by Rand McNally & Company.

Yale University Press for "Chanticleer" by John Farrar from *Songs For Parents*. Reprinted by permission of Yale University Press.

The Swallows

Nine swallows sat on a telephone wire:
"Teeter, teeter," and then they were still,
all facing one way, with the sun like a fire
along their blue shoulders, and hot on each bill.
But they sat there so quietly, all of the nine,
that I almost forgot they were swallows at all.
They seemed more like clothespins left out on
  the line
when the wash is just dried, and the first rain-
  drops fall.

Elizabeth Coatsworth

Sunning

Old Dog lay in the summer sun
Much too lazy to rise and run.
He flapped an ear
At a buzzing fly;
He winked a half-opened
Sleepy eye;
He scratched himself
On an itching spot;
As he dozed on the porch
When the sun was hot.
He whimpered a bit
From force of habit,
While he lazily dreamed
Of chasing a rabbit.
But Old Dog happily lay in the sun,
Much too lazy to rise and run.

James S. Tippett

Cat

The black cat yawns,
Opens her jaws,
Stretches her legs,
And shows her claws.

Then she gets up
And stands on four
Long stiff legs
And yawns some more.

She shows her sharp teeth,
She stretches her lip,
Her slice of a tongue
Turns up at the tip.

Lifting herself
On her delicate toes,
She arches her back
As high as it goes.

She lets herself down
With particular care,
And pads away
With her tail in the air.

Mary Britton Miller

The Rabbit

Brown bunny sits inside his burrow
Till everything is still,
Then out he slips along the furrow,
Or up the grassy hill.

He nibbles all about the bushes
Or sits to wash his face—
But at a sound he stamps and rushes
At a surprising pace—

You see some little streaks and flashes—
A last sharp twink of white

As down his hidy-hole he dashes—
And disappears from sight.

Edith King

Opossum

Have you ever in your life seen a Possum play possum?
Have you ever in your life seen a Possum play dead?
When a Possum is trapped and can't get away
He turns up his toes and lays down his head,
Bats both his eyes and rolls over dead.
But then when you leave him and run off to play,
The Possum that really was just playing possum
Gets up in a flash and scurries away.

William Jay Smith

Oriole

See my pretty little nest,
    Built of bits of string;
When the breezes whisper near,
    You should see it swing!
There are four wee babies there,
    In that silken cradle,
They'll sing grown-up Oriole songs,
    Soon as they are able.

Marion Mitchell Walker

The Squirrel

Whisky, frisky,
Hippity hop.
Up he goes
To the tree top!

Whirly, twirly,
Round and round,
Down he scampers
To the ground.

Furly, curly,
What a tail!
Tall as a feather,
Broad as a sail!

Where's his supper?
In the shell,
Snappity, crackity,
Out it fell!

Anonymous

Mrs. Peck-Pigeon

Mrs. Peck-Pigeon
Is picking for bread,
Bob-bob-bob
Goes her little round head.
Tame as a pussy-cat
In the street,
Step-step-step
Go her little red feet.
With her little red feet
And her little round head,
Mrs. Peck-Pigeon
Goes picking for bread.

Eleanor Farjeon

The Ducks

When our ducks waddle to the pond,
They're awkward as awkward can be—
But when they get in the water and swim,
They glide most gracefully.

Alice Wilkins

Chanticleer

High and proud on the barnyard fence
Walks rooster in the morning.
He shakes his comb, he shakes his tail
And gives his daily warning.

Get up, you lazy boys and girls,
It's time you should be dressing.
I wonder if he keeps a clock,
Or is he only guessing?

John Farrar

The Cow

The friendly cow all red and white,
   I love with all my heart:
She gives me cream with all her might,
   To eat with apple-tart.

She wanders lowing here and there,
   And yet she cannot stray,
All in the pleasant open air,
   The pleasant light of day;

And blown by all the winds that pass
   And wet with all the showers,
She walks among the meadow grass
   And eats the meadow flowers.

Robert Louis Stevenson

Mice and Cat

One mouse, two mice,
Three mice, four,
Stealing from their tunnel,
Creeping through the door.

Softly! Softly!
Don't make a sound—
Don't let your little feet
Patter on the ground.

There on the hearthrug,
Sleek and fat,
Soundly sleeping,
Lies old Tom Cat.

If he should hear you,
There'd be no more
Of one mouse, two mice,
Three mice, four.

So please be careful
How far you roam,
For if you should wake him...
He'd-chase-you-all-HOME!

Clive Sansom

The Snow-Bird

When all the ground with snow is white,
　　The merry snow-bird comes,
And hops about with great delight
　　To find the scattered crumbs.

How glad he seems to get to eat
　　A piece of cake or bread!
He wears no shoes upon his feet,
　　Nor hat upon his head.

But happiest is he, I know,
　　Because no cage with bars
Keeps him from walking on the snow
　　And printing it with stars.

Frank Dempster Sherman

Birds in the Garden

Greedy little sparrow,
    Great big crow,
Saucy little chickadee,
    All in a row.

Are you very hungry,
    No place to go?
Come and eat my breadcrumbs,
    In the snow.

Anonymous

What Will Robin Do?

The north wind doth blow,
And we shall have snow,
And what will the robin do then,
    Poor thing?

He'll sit in the barn,
And keep himself warm,
And hide his head under his wing,
    Poor thing!

Old English Song

Foal

Come trotting up
Beside your mother,
Little skinny.

Lay your neck across
Her back, and whinny,
Little foal.

You think you're a horse
Because you can trot—
But you're not.

Your eyes are so wild,
And each leg is as tall
As a pole;

And you're only a skittish
Child, after all,
Little foal.

Mary Britton Miller

The Donkey

I saw a donkey
One day old,
His head was too big
For his neck to hold;
His legs were shaky
And long and loose,
They rocked and staggered
And weren't much use.

He tried to gambol
And frisk a bit,
But he wasn't quite sure
Of the trick of it.
His queer little coat
Was soft and grey,
And curled at his neck
In a lovely way.

His face was wistful
And left no doubt
That he felt life needed
Some thinking about.
So he blundered round
In venturesome quest,
And then lay flat
On the ground to rest.

He looked so little
And weak and slim,
I prayed the world
Might be good to him.

Anonymous

Crickets

What makes the crickets "crick" all night
    And never stop to rest?
They must take naps in daytime
    So at night they'll "crick" their best.
I wonder if they just take turns
    And try to make it rhyme,
Or do a million crickets
    Keep "cricking" all the time?

Helen Wing

The Happy Sheep

All through the night the happy sheep
Lie in the meadow grass asleep.

Their wool keeps out the frost and rain
Until the sun comes round again.

They have no buttons to undo,
Nor hair to brush like me and you,

And with the light they lift their heads
To find their breakfast on their beds

Or rise and walk about and eat
The carpet underneath their feet.

Wilfred Thorley

Firefly

A SONG

A little light is going by,
Is going up to see the sky,
A little light with wings.

I never could have thought of it,
To have a little bug all lit
And made to go on wings.

Elizabeth Madox Roberts

Snail

Little snail,
Dreaming you go.
Weather and rose
Is all you know.

Weather and rose
Is all you see,
Drinking
The dewdrop's
Mystery.

Langston Hughes

The Turtle

The turtle's always been inclined
to live within his shell.
But why he cares to be confined,
the turtle does not tell.

The turtle's always satisfied
to slowly creep and crawl,
and never wanders far outside
his living room or hall.

So if you wish to visit him
in his domestic dome,
just knock politely on his shell,
you'll find the turtle home.

Jack Prelutsky